COOKING

SECRETS

pil

Publications International, Ltd.

ISBN-13: 978-1-4127-2640-5
ISBN-10: 1-4127-2640-9

Manufactured in China.

8 7 6 5 4 3 2 1

CONTENTS

What the Kitchen Pros Know • 5

Food Smarts • 6

Fish & Seafood ✦ Fruits ✦ Meats ✦ Vegetables

Cooking Know-How • 51

Baking, Roasting & Braising ✦ Boiling,
Simmering & Poaching ✦ Broiling ✦ Frying ✦
Grilling ✦ Microwaving ✦ Seasoning

Baking Wisdom • 66

Bakeware ✦ Breads, Muffins & Biscuits ✦
Cakes ✦ Cookies & Brownies ✦ Ingredients ✦
Pies & Pastries

WHAT THE KITCHEN PROS KNOW

There are plenty of cookbooks on the shelves and sites on the Web that can provide you with recipes and even with step-by-step instructions for accomplishing various cooking tasks. Harder to find are the tips, tricks, and fixes—the hard-won know-how that comes from experience—that can make your time in the kitchen more efficient, effective, and enjoyable. *Cooking Secrets* is your little treasury of expert tactics for preventing or solving the many minor frustrations and failures everyone faces in the kitchen. Here you'll find keys to choosing, storing, and preparing the freshest and most flavorful foods; clues to smart cooking on the stove, in the oven, on the grill, and in the microwave; and little-known tricks that can help ensure baking success. With this collection of culinary inside information, you'll save yourself time, money, and misery and rediscover the true joy that cooking good food can bring.

FOOD SMARTS

Professional chefs and seasoned cooks alike know that the real key to preparing memorable, mouth-watering dishes and scrumptious, satisfying meals lies in paying careful attention to the quality of the ingredients. Through years of experience, they have discovered the secrets to spotting the juiciest, ripest pieces of fruit; the crunchiest, most flavorful vegetables; and the freshest meat, poultry, and fish. They've learned, too, how best to store and work with individual foods to preserve and highlight each one's culinary qualities. These mavens of the kitchen know that trying to work with poor ingredients is a waste of time, energy, and money and can doom even the most tried-and-true recipe. Now you, too, can benefit from their accumulated wisdom. This chapter reveals the secrets experienced cooks use to select, store, and prepare the tastiest, highest-quality foods.

Fish & Seafood

- Buy only fresh fish. Do not buy fish that smells fishy. It should be firm, not soft, to the touch; the scales should be shiny and clean, not slimy; and the eyes should be clear, not cloudy, and bulging, not sunken. Fillets and steaks should look moist, not dried or curled at the edges.

- When buying shellfish in the shells, be sure the shells are tightly closed. If a shell is slightly open, tap it lightly; it should snap shut. If it doesn't, the creature is dead and should be discarded.

- Don't buy crabs that have slimy or greasy shells.

- Discard mushy shrimp immediately.

- It's best to cook fresh fish the day you buy it, but it will keep in the refrigerator overnight if placed in a plastic bag over a bowl of ice. To store it any longer, freeze it.

- The quality of fish is better retained if it is frozen quickly, so freeze whole fish only if it weighs two pounds or less. Larger fish should be cut into pieces, steaks, or fillets for freezing.

- Lean fish will keep in the freezer up to six months; fatty fish, only about three months.

- Never refreeze fish that has been previously frozen and thawed.

- Always thaw frozen fish in the refrigerator, not at room temperature.

- Store live shellfish in the refrigerator for no more than 24 hours. Keep them moist with a damp paper towel, but be sure they can breathe through it.

Fruits

- Since most fruits are eaten raw, the secret to serving delicious fruit is to make sure the pieces you serve are ripe, when their taste and texture are at their peak.

- Use stainless-steel knives to cut fruit; carbon-steel knives can react with fruit and cause unsightly discoloration.

- To peel thick-skinned fruit easily, put the fruit in a bowl, pour boiling water over it, and wait one minute. Remove the fruit with tongs, and peel the skin with a sharp paring knife.

- To prevent freshly cut fruit such as apples and pears from turning brown, keep the fruit submerged in "lemon water," a mixture of six parts water to one part lemon juice.

One Bad Apple...

You've probably heard the saying that "One bad apple can spoil the whole bunch." It's a good warning to remember—and one that applies to many other kinds of fruit, as well. So whenever possible, select pieces of fruit one by one rather than buying them in prepackaged bunches. The packaging can hide rotten spots and damaged or moldy fruit. And even one moldy or rotten piece in a package can speed up spoilage of the remaining fruit. (It's also important to monitor fruit once you bring it home so you can quickly weed out any spoiled pieces.)

Apples

- Choose firm apples with few blemishes, and look for those with "bloom" (a dusky coating), not a fake, waxy shine.

- Store apples in clear plastic or mesh rather than a paper bag, so you can easily spot any that are spoiling and remove them before they contaminate the others.

- Apples like humidity, so store them in the refrigerator crisper drawer, where they'll keep for two to three weeks.

- If you don't have lemon juice, you can maintain the crispness of apple slices and prevent browning by immersing them in saltwater for ten minutes before you use them.

- To prevent apples from shrinking when you bake them, remove a horizontal belt of peel from around the middle of each one.

- To keep apples from wrinkling during baking, cut random slits in each apple before placing them in the oven.

Apricots

- You'll find the freshest tree-ripened apricots in June and July.

- Choose fragrant, plump, golden-orange fruit that yields to slight pressure; hard, yellowish, or green-tinged fruit was picked too early. However, because fresh apricots are delicate, they're often sold unripe. Allow these to ripen at home at room temperature. Store ripe apricots in the refrigerator; they'll keep about a week.

- To avoid bruising, don't pile ripe apricots on top of one another.

Avocados

- You can purchase the California Haas, a small, dark, pebbly-skinned avocado with oily flesh, year-round. But its bigger Florida cousin, a bright-green avocado with smooth skin and juicier, less oily flesh, is only in season in late summer and fall.

- Choose a heavy avocado that yields to slight pressure but isn't too soft. (If necessary, you can bring a harder one home and let it ripen at room temperature.) If it's a Florida avocado, it will still be green even when it's ripe; Haas avocados turn a purply-black color when they're ripe.

Bananas

- Choose green or ripe bananas as your taste and needs dictate, but keep in mind that bananas get sweeter and softer as they ripen.

- Keep unripened bananas at room temperature. Ripe bananas can be stored in the refrigerator;

the skin will turn black, but they will be fine on the inside for another few days.

Berries

- Nearly all berries are fragile and perishable; handle them with care.

- Select berries that are firm but not hard.

- If you can't select your berries individually, look at the bottom of the container: If it is wet or stained, much of the fruit within it is probably mushy or moldy.

- If you've bought prepackaged berries, examine each one when you get them home. Remove any bruised or spoiled berries, because mold spreads quickly from berry to berry.

- To keep berries in prime condition, don't wash them until you are ready to eat them.

- Refrigerate berries in a colander to allow air circulation that will help prevent mold.

- **Blackberries** grow on thorny shrubs and are extremely fragile. Their peak months are June, July, and August; that's when you'll find the best blackberries at the best prices. Look for blackberries that are glossy, plump, round, deeply colored, and firm. The darker the berries, the riper and sweeter they are. Refrigerate them unwashed,

Berry Interesting

Blackberries are often confused with black raspberries and related hybrids. The loganberry is a cross between a blackberry and a raspberry. The boysenberry is a crossing of a blackberry, a raspberry, and a loganberry.

and use them within a day or so. Do not overhandle blackberries—their cells will break open and they will lose juice and nutrients—but do remove stems and berries that are too soft. Wash them gently under running water and drain well before eating. You can also freeze them: Rinse and dry them thoroughly, arrange them in a single layer on a baking sheet, cover, and freeze. Once they are frozen, place them in airtight containers, then thaw them as needed.

- **Blueberries** are either wild or commercial. Wild blueberries, which are much smaller and more flavorful than commercial berries, are available only in certain parts of the country because they are very perishable. Whether you're buying wild or commercial, look for plump berries with a good blue color and a powdery "bloom" (a natural protective coating produced by the berry itself). If you're lucky enough to find wild blueberries, use them immediately or pack clean, dry wild blueberries in freezer containers and freeze them for later use in baking. Commercial blueberries can be refrigerated in their original container (remove any mushy berries first), where they'll usually last for five to seven days. Like their wild siblings, commercial blueberries can be frozen and stored for use out of season. Be sure to rinse all blueberries gently and remove any stems before eating, using, or freezing.

- **Raspberries** are very fragile, so choose and use them with care, and eat them as soon as possible. Look for brightly colored berries with no hulls attached; if the green hulls are still on the berries, the berries will be tart. Avoid any that look shriveled or have visible mold. They should be plump, firm, well shaped, and evenly colored, with no green. They should be packed in a single-layer container and have a clean, slightly sweet fragrance. When you get them home, chill the unwashed berries in the refrigerator for no more than a day before using, or rinse, dry, and freeze them for longer storage. Just before serving the chilled raspberries, rinse them under cool running water. For recipes that require the juice to be separated from frozen raspberries, thaw the raspberries in a strainer that is set over a bowl.

- **Strawberries** come in a wide assortment. Many shoppers have a tendency to reach for huge, bright-red, well-shaped strawberries, but the flavor of these perfect-looking berries does not always match their outer beauty (although thanks to new breeding techniques, "big" doesn't always mean "tasteless" anymore). Often, smaller berries have a sweeter, more distinct strawberry flavor. Choose berries that are deep red all over with bright-green leafy caps and a sweet, ripe smell. Avoid berries that are too soft, and be sure to check prepackaged strawberries as carefully as you can for mold. Strawberries should be stored unwashed in the refrigerator, with their caps attached, until ready to use. Use as soon as possible (preferably within a day or two), and rinse gently just before serving. Always be sure to hull (cut the caps off) strawberries only after they are washed, or they will absorb some of the water, causing the fruit to become mushy. If a recipe calls for coarsely crushed strawberries, try using a potato masher.

Cherries

- The best and least-expensive cherries can generally be found from about mid-June to mid-August, when they are in season.

- Sweet cherries should be plump and firm with a bright color that may be red, yellow tinged with red, or reddish-brown to black, depending on the variety. Avoid buying immature fruit—which is hard, smaller, and light in color—or cherries that are overly soft.

Hide the Evidence!

Baking, cooking, or preparing homemade preserves with berries, cherries, or similar fruits can leave you with stained fingers that regular soap just can't fix. To help remove the color, try rinsing your hands with lemon juice or soaking a paper towel or cloth in lemon juice and gently rubbing away the stains.

To remove a fruit, juice, or wine stain from a countertop, cover it with a thick layer of baking soda, sprinkle on lemon juice, and wait several minutes before gently scrubbing the area with a damp cloth. You may have to repeat this a second time for darker stains.

Another way to tackle fruit juice and even coffee or tea stains on pots, pans, countertops, and other kitchen surfaces is to squeeze some toothpaste (the gel type may not work as well) on an old toothbrush, moisten the paste slightly, and gently scrub the area until the stain fades away.

- Check cherries at the market for cuts or sticky leaks, as they generally mean that other cherries in the batch are also going bad. One bad cherry will eventually ruin the whole bunch.

- Choose cherries that still have their stems attached. A missing stem makes the fruit more vulnerable to spoilage. The stem should be green and pliable, not brown and brittle.

- Cherries are ready to wash and eat or use when you buy them; they will not continue to ripen off the vine.

- Choose cherries that have been kept cool and moist, because as the temperature rises, their flavor and texture suffer. When you get them home, check for and remove any bad cherries, then keep the rest refrigerated in a covered container. Use them within a few days.

- Fresh sweet cherries can be frozen for later enjoyment—a good thing to remember since their growing season is so short. Simply wash the fruit, remove the stems and pits and any bad cherries, drain well, and place in a plastic bag. They'll keep in the freezer up to a year.

- Pie and sauce recipes typically call for *sour* cherries, not the sweet cherries you eat out of hand. Recipes that call for sour cherries always include sugar or some other sweetener, because they are too tart to be eaten without it.

Grapefruit

- Look for firm, smooth, thin-skinned grapefruit that feel heavy for their size; they will be the juiciest. Avoid soft or mushy fruit.

- Skip grapefruit that are oblong rather than round; they are generally of poorer quality (possibly pithy and less sweet).

- Grapefruit is not picked until it is ripe, because it will not continue to ripen off the vine. So,

Pink or White, Just as Nice

Despite what many shoppers think, there is no significant difference in taste between white and pink (or red) grapefruit. White grapefruit has yellowish flesh inside, and pink grapefruit has pink or pinkish-red flesh, but all are equally sweet (and equally tart).

unless you plan to use the grapefruit within a couple days of purchase, it will last longer if you refrigerate it once you get it home. Refrigerated grapefruit will keep for two to three weeks or more.

- Unlike some other foods, grapefruit does best in the warmest part of your refrigerator, which is usually the vegetable crisper.

- For greater juiciness and flavor, remove the grapefruit from the refrigerator and allow it to reach room temperature before eating or juicing.

- Be sure to wash grapefruit before you cut it to prevent any bacteria on the outside from being introduced inside.

- Despite claims made by promoters of so-called grapefruit diets, grapefruit does not cause the body to burn fat or excess calories. However, because it is high in filling fiber and other nutrients, low in calories, and basically fat free, grapefruit can be a valuable asset to a healthy weight-loss plan.

Grapes

- The peak season for the most popular variety of grapes, Thompson seedless, is June through November, although you should be able to find some variety of fresh grapes throughout the year.

- Grapes become sweet as they ripen on the vine, but once harvested, they will not ripen further. So if you sample a bunch before purchasing and the grape is too sour for your taste, do not buy the bunch hoping the rest will get sweeter.

- When choosing grapes, look for clusters of plump, firm fruit that are securely attached to pliable green stems. Soft or wrinkled grapes, grapes that have bleached areas around the stem, and grapes that fall easily from the bunch are past their prime.

- Good color is the key to good flavor in grapes. The sweetest green grapes are yellow-green in color. Among the red variety, those that are predominantly crimson-red, with no sign of green, will have the best flavor. And blue-black grapes taste best if their color is deep and rich, almost black, without pale or greenish spots.

- When you get grapes home, immediately store them, unwashed, in a perforated plastic bag in the refrigerator, where they'll keep for up to a week. Just before serving grapes, rinse the clusters, drain them, and pat them dry. If you rinse grapes before you store them in the refrigerator, they will turn soft more quickly.

Kiwifruit

- Choose kiwi that are fairly firm but that give under slight pressure. Avoid kiwi that are soft or have dark areas; it usually means they've been bruised or they're overripe.

- Unripe kiwi can have a strong, sour taste, but fortunately, they will continue to ripen if unrefrigerated. Allow firm kiwi about a week to ripen at room temperature.

- You can hasten ripening by placing kiwi in a paper bag. Try adding an apple or banana to the bag, too, since ripening apples and bananas emit a gas that speeds ripening of kiwi and other fruit.

- Ripe kiwi should be stored in the refrigerator, where they will last for one to two weeks. Place them in the fruit bin away from other fruits so they don't absorb unwanted flavors.

- The skin of kiwifruit is edible if you rub off the brown fuzz; however, most people prefer to peel kiwi before eating. If a kiwi is ripe, its core is edible, too.

- Raw kiwi contains an enzyme that makes a great meat tenderizer. You can cut a kiwi in half and rub it over the meat before cooking, and it won't alter the flavor of the meat.

- The same enzyme in kiwi that makes it a good meat tenderizer also makes it impossible for gelatin to set if raw kiwi has been added to it.

Lemons & Limes

- For the juiciest, most flavorful lemons and limes, choose those that are heavy for their size, with thin, smooth skins and small points at each end.

- To encourage lemons and limes to yield more juice, put them—uncut—in the refrigerator in a tightly sealed container of water as soon as you get them home. They will usually keep for a month or two.

- You'll also get more juice from lemons and limes if you warm them to room temperature just prior to use and roll them on the countertop with the palm of your hand before squeezing them.

- If you need only a small amount of juice, make a hole in the lemon or lime with a toothpick,  squeeze out the amount you need, seal the hole by reinserting the toothpick, and store the fruit in the refrigerator.

- The easiest way to remove strips of lemon or lime peel—also known as the zest—is to use a potato peeler or lemon zester. Be sure to remove only the colored part of the peel and not the white inner layer, which is very bitter. Strip off any white attached to the peel before adding the peel to your recipe.

- If you plan to use both the juice and peel from a lemon or lime, grate the peel first, then squeeze out the juice.

- Limes take on a yellowish color as they ripen on the vine, but very green limes have the best flavor. Once limes have been picked, they will not ripen further. Sunlight will cause them to yellow, however, so protect them from exposure.

Melons

- In general, look for melons that are evenly shaped and have no bruises, cuts, or soft spots.

Shaking a Myth

Some people say that to determine the ripeness of a melon, you need to thump it and listen for a specific sound. Others say you need to shake it—presumably to hear the juice sloshing around. So which of these two methods really works? Neither. Thumping and shaking and most other traditional techniques do not provide an accurate indication of a melon's ripeness. The best clues can be found in the rind. (See the discussion of each melon variety on the following pages to learn what rind attributes to look for.)

- A melon that has reached peak ripeness or has been cut should be refrigerated and used within a couple days or so.

- All melons taste better slightly chilled than at room temperature, but watermelons taste best when they're ice-cold.

- When storing melons, do not remove the seeds, even if you cut the fruit, until you're ready to serve. The seeds help keep the melon moist.

- **Cantaloupes** are available year-round, but their peak season is June through October. Cantaloupes should have a prominent brown netting that stands out from the underlying smooth skin and covers the entire surface; if there are areas of rind without this netting, choose a different one. The rind beneath the netting should have a slight gold color; skip those that have a dull green rind. There should be a depressed area on the end where the stem used to be; don't buy a cantaloupe that still has its stem attached, because that means it was picked too early. A ripe cantaloupe should give off a mildly sweet fragrance (unless it's chilled, which mutes the fragrance); if it smells sickeningly sweet or if there is mold where the stem used to be, it is overripe and may well be rotten. Select cantaloupes that are heavy for their size; they tend to be juiciest.

- **Honeydew melons** are generally available year-round, but August and September are really the peak months for them. Look for a honeydew with an off-white or yellowish-white rind, which tells you that the melon is ripe. Avoid those that are completely white or greenish white. If the rind is green, the melon will never ripen. If the rind is smooth, that also generally means that the melon was picked prematurely; the rind should instead have a very slight wrinkled feel. Ripe honeydews are the sweetest of the melons, and the largest honeydews are typically the best tasting. Although honeydews keep longer than cantaloupes, they should still be refrigerated. A whole honeydew will last up to four or five days in the refrigerator.

- **Watermelons** are at their peak from mid-June to late August, although they're in season March through October. As watermelons ripen on the vine, they develop a creamy yellow underbelly, which is probably the single most reliable indicator that a watermelon is ripe. If the underside is white or green, the melon is not yet mature. You should also select a melon that is firm to the touch. Watermelons don't ripen much after they are picked, so if possible, refrigerate the whole melon once you bring it home; it will keep up to a week.

Nectarines

- Nectarines are available from late spring to early fall but are best in midsummer.

- Buy nectarines that are fairly ripe: They should not be rock hard, just a bit yielding to the touch along the seam, and should have a hint of aroma. Avoid nectarines with bruises, cuts, or pinholes.

- A green-tinged nectarine was picked too early and won't ripen. And a red blush isn't a sign of ripeness, just of the variety.

- A nectarine that is not quite ripe can be placed in a ventilated paper bag at room temperature for two or three days to ripen. If it doesn't, it was picked too early, in which case it will continue to soften (and get mealy) but will never become sweet.

- Refrigerate fully ripe nectarines and use them within a day or two. For best flavor, allow them to reach room temperature just prior to eating.

A Slimmer "Peach Pie"
By substituting nectarines in any pie or cobbler recipe that calls for peaches, you can use half the sugar and fat called for in the recipe and not affect the end product's flavor.

Oranges & Tangerines

- Choose fruit that is firm to the touch and feels heavy for its size, indicating juiciness.

- A green color and occasional blemishes do not indicate lack of ripeness or poor quality; only fully ripened fruit is picked.

- **Oranges,** if refrigerated loose, will keep for up to two weeks. They will last almost as long if kept at room temperature, however, and will be juicier.

- **Tangerines,** which are simply a type of mandarin orange, are more delicate: They should be refrigerated, handled with care, and eaten within a few days of purchase.

Peaches

- Peaches have a fairly long season, mid-spring to mid-fall, but they're at their peak in the summer. Imported peaches are often available in winter.

- Always pick peaches individually, carefully checking for and rejecting those that have blemishes or bruises.

- Choose plump, well-shaped fruit with a creamy, golden color and a well-defined crease. A green undertone is a sure sign that the peach is not ripe, although a blush simply indicates variety, not ripeness.

- Avoid rock-hard peaches; they were picked too soon to ripen off the tree. Instead, select those that are soft along the seam, but don't squeeze them, because they bruise and decay quite easily.

- Slightly underripe peaches will ripen further if kept at room temperature in a ventilated paper bag. Don't let them get overripe, though, because they'll be mealy.

- A peach is ripe when just soft and when you can smell a sweet aroma.

- It's best to eat ripe peaches right away, but they will keep for a few days if refrigerated; just bring them to room temperature prior to eating.

- To easily peel peaches for pies or other desserts, put them in boiling water for 10 to 20 seconds, then run them under ice-cold water, and peel.

Pears

- Pears become mealy if left on the tree to ripen, so they're picked before they're ripe. Off the tree, their starch starts to turn into sugar. Once they're ripe, they are easily bruised and, unless refrigerated, turn rotten quickly. So it's best to buy unripe pears a few days before you need them and ripen them at home, at room temperature, in a ventilated paper bag. When ripe, eat them or refrigerate them for no more than a day or two.

- You can't always tell if a pear is ripe by its color; besides, pears ripen from the inside out, so once the outside looks perfect, the inside may be starting to rot. Touch is a better indicator. Buy those that are firm but not rock hard, and eat them when they just barely yield to gentle pressure.

- When ripening pears or when storing ripe ones, do not pile them on top of one another and do not let them sit on one side too long, because they bruise very easily.

Pineapples

- When shopping for a pineapple, let your nose be your guide to ripeness. Forget all the other tricks you've heard. A ripe pineapple emits a sweet aroma from its base, except when cold. It should not smell sour or fermented. Color is not a reliable guide, because ripe pineapples vary in hue. And don't rely on plucking a leaf from the middle; you can do this with all but the most unripe pineapples, and it can just as easily mean the fruit is rotten.

- Shop for a large pineapple that feels heavy for its size, indicating juiciness and a lot of pulp. Avoid rock-hard pineapples and those with surface

Pineapple's Hidden Talent

Fresh pineapple contains an enzyme that breaks down protein, so you can use the fruit to tenderize meat. Next time you marinate a steak or other cut of meat, add chunks of fresh pineapple to your marinade, and let it sit for ten minutes. Don't keep the meat in the pineapple marinade longer than that, though, or your meat will turn mushy. And don't try this with canned pineapple, since it doesn't contain the tenderizing enzyme. (That's why you can add canned pineapple to gelatin without difficulty, but if you add fresh pineapple, the enzyme will keep the gelatin from setting.)

damage; a ripe pineapple should yield slightly when pressed. The leaves should be smallish and vivid green, not brown or wilted. The eyes should stand out, not be sunken.

- It's best to eat a ripe pineapple the day you buy it, since it will not continue to ripen or turn any sweeter. Otherwise, put it in the refrigerator and eat it as soon as you can.

Plums

- Look for a plump plum that has a bright or deep color and is covered with a powdery "bloom"— its natural protection. If it yields to gentle palm pressure, it's ripe. If not, as long as it is not rock hard, it will ripen at home—but it won't get sweeter, just softer.

- To ripen plums, place them in a loosely closed paper bag at room temperature. Check them frequently, and eat or refrigerate them as soon as they become slightly soft.

- Don't wash plums until just before you eat them; you'll remove the fruit's protective "bloom."

Tomatoes

- Although fresh tomatoes are available year-round, their peak season is June to September.

- The most flavorful tomatoes are "vine ripened," that is, they have been allowed to become ripe on the vine rather than being picked green and treated. You may need to shop farmer's markets or green grocers for them or grow your own.

- Choose evenly red tomatoes that are firm and well shaped and have a noticeable, fresh fragrance. They should be heavy for their size and yield to slight pressure when gently squeezed.

- You can also opt for paler, salmon-colored tomatoes or even mature green tomatoes and ripen them at home—just be sure they have a mild tomato aroma even at their not-yet-ripe stage (no aroma means they were

Can I See Some ID?

Although the tomato is related to the potato, the bell pepper, and the eggplant and is thought of by many folks as a vegetable (remember when the government classified ketchup in school lunch programs as a serving of vegetables?), it is botanically classified as a fruit.

 probably picked too early to ever ripen properly). Ripen them at home by placing them in a single layer, along with an apple or banana, in a paper bag at room temperature.

- A common mistake is to store tomatoes in the refrigerator. Cold temperatures ruin the taste and texture of a good tomato. Tomatoes that are ripe should be kept at room temperature, out of the sun, and should be eaten within a couple of days.

- To peel tomatoes, place them, one at a time, in a saucepan of simmering water for about ten seconds. (Add about 30 seconds if they are not fully ripened.) Then immediately plunge them into cold water for ten seconds. The skin will peel off easily with a knife. Do not put more than one tomato at a time into the simmering water; if you do, the water temperature will drop rapidly and the tomatoes will stew before their skins can be removed.

Dressing Too Early?
Refrain from slicing and tossing cut tomatoes into a salad until just before serving, because once the tomatoes are cut, they begin losing their juice and flavor. Adding salt or a salty dressing to the salad ahead of time will drain even more juice from the cut tomatoes.

- To heighten the flavor of cooked tomatoes, add a pinch of sugar to the cooking water.

- Cut tomatoes from top (stem end) to bottom rather than from side to side to retain more juice in the slices.

- Slice tomatoes only when you're ready to serve them; once cut, their flavor begins to fade.

Meats

- Thaw meats in the refrigerator (allow about five hours per pound) or microwave (follow the manufacturer's directions), not at room temperature.

- Never freeze meat that was previously frozen and then thawed but not cooked.

Beef

- Choose beef that looks evenly red and not dried out. If it's turning brown, it's not fresh.

- Refrigerate (or freeze) all beef as soon as you get it home. Place it on a plate in the refrigerator so that drippings do not contaminate other foods.

- If you don't plan on using ground beef within 24 hours of purchase, freeze it as soon as you get it home.

- Freeze any cuts of beef that you do not plan to use within three or four days of purchase.

Refrigerator Wisdom

You may have noticed that some food-storage secrets refer to the "coldest" or "warmest" part of your refrigerator. Meat, for example, should be kept in the coldest part. And while the latest refrigerator models tend to do a better job of stabilizing temperatures, all fridges are likely to have cold and warm spots. So to keep your food fresh and safe, you need to identify the warm and cold spots in your fridge and make sure the temperatures inside never leave the safety zone. Your fridge's manual may provide information on this, but the best approach is to use a refrigerator thermometer (check your local hardware or appliance store). Measure the temperature at various levels and positions (front, center, and back of each shelf) in the fridge, including any crisper and meat drawers. All the readings should fall between 32°F and 40°F. If any are above 40 degrees, turn down the appliance's thermostat to avoid spoilage and bacterial growth. Readings below 32°F mean food stored in those areas is at risk of ice-crystal formation and freezing. Make note of the warmest and coolest areas in your fridge. Then be sure to keep the thermometer in the fridge—moving it to a different spot occasionally—so you can continue to monitor your fridge's temperatures and keep your edibles safe and fresh.

Pork

- When shopping for fresh pork, choose cuts that are pink (with the exception of tenderloin, which should be red), perhaps with a slight gray tinge, and well-trimmed of fat. The ends of the bones should be red; white-tipped bones suggest an older animal with tougher meat.

- All pork must be thoroughly cooked to kill trichinae parasites that may be present; the parasites cause a serious infection in humans.

- Bacon will keep in the refrigerator for no more than about ten days or can be frozen for up to three months.

- Freeze pork chops and roasts if you don't plan to cook them within two to three days of purchase.

- Fully cooked hams and even canned hams should be refrigerated (check the label for storage instructions). Packaged ham slices should be stored in the coldest part of the refrigerator. Use ham slices within three or four days and whole hams within a week.

- Ham does not freeze well.

Veal

- Choose veal that's pinkish in color and has very little fatty marbling.

- Use veal within one to two days of purchase.

- Because veal is so delicate, nearly all cuts benefit from roasting, sautéing, or braising at a low temperature.

- To keep veal from curling during cooking, remove any visible fat.

Poultry (Chicken & Turkey)

- Avoid poultry with bruised or dry-looking skin.

- Avoid frozen poultry with ice crystals in its packaging; they are a sign of freezer burn.

- Fresh (unfrozen), raw poultry—whether whole or in pieces—will keep in the coldest part of the refrigerator for up to two days. Be sure to place a dish, platter, or other protection under it to prevent juices from contaminating other foods. Fresh, raw pieces that you will not cook within two days should be placed in the freezer. If you plan to purchase a whole bird but cannot cook it within two days, either cut it into pieces and freeze the pieces in smaller packages or buy a whole bird that is already frozen and put it in your home freezer. (Typical home freezers will not freeze an entire bird fast enough to prevent potentially dangerous bacterial growth.)

- To properly freeze poultry pieces, remove them from their original packaging, rinse them under cold water, pat them dry with paper towels, and divide them into separate packages that you wrap in freezer paper, label with the date, and place in the freezer. Frozen poultry pieces will keep up to six months in the freezer.

- When shopping for a frozen, whole bird, look for one that is frozen solid, with wrapping that is well sealed and intact and with no ice crystals inside the package. A frozen, whole bird that you do not plan to defrost and use right away should be put in the freezer as soon as you get it home. Whole, frozen birds will typically keep up to eight months (chicken) or a year (turkey) after purchase (less if it sat in the store for months first).

- To defrost chicken, thaw it in its wrapping in the refrigerator (never at room temperature), with a plate beneath it to catch juices; allow about three to four hours per pound.

Vegetables

Asparagus

- Asparagus season runs from February through July.

- Look for fresh asparagus with a bright-green color; stalks that are smooth, firm, straight, and round, not flat; and tips that are compact, closed, pointed, and purplish in color. Avoid sandy stalks, as the sand is very difficult to wash out. Thick stalks are fine; they don't indicate toughness in this case.

- Try to choose stalks of similar size, so they will finish cooking at about the same time.

- Wrap fresh asparagus loosely in a plastic bag and keep refrigerated. It will last almost a week but won't taste as good after a day or so.

- To enjoy asparagus year-round, blanch it the day you buy it, wrap it tightly in foil, and freeze for up to 12 months.

- Just before cooking, bend each spear until the stem end snaps off; discard stem.

- Avoid overcooking asparagus. When cooked to crisp-tender, it'll be bright green; overcooked, it turns an unappealing green and becomes floppy. Simmer three to five minutes only. Or, for more even cooking, stand the stalks upright in boiling water, with the tips sticking out of the water, for five to ten minutes; the tips will be steamed as the stalks cook. Microwaving will take two to three minutes in a dish with a quarter cup water.

Beets

- Beets are in stores year-round, but their peak season is June through October.

- Choose small, firm, well-rounded beets of uniform size for even cooking. Skins should be deep red, smooth, and unblemished. A clue to tenderness is a thin taproot (the root that extends from the bulb). The freshest beets are those with bright, crisp greens on top.

- Once you get beets home, immediately cut off the greens, which suck moisture from the beet, but leave two inches of stem to prevent "bleeding" during cooking. Don't trim the taproot.

- Refrigerated, beets will keep for a week or two.

- Wash fresh beets gently, so you don't break the skin and allow color and nutrients to escape.

- To retain beets' color and nutrients, peel them only after they're cooked.

- Microwaving retains the most nutrients. Steaming is okay but takes 25 to 45 minutes. Beets are done when a fork easily pierces the skin.

- Use caution when working with beets: Their powerful pigment easily stains cutting boards and nonmetal utensils.

Broccoli & Cauliflower

- Both are available year-round, but their quality is lower and cost higher in summer.

- Steaming is the cooking method that'll preserve the most nutrients and flavor. Steam only until crisp-tender (broccoli should be bright green); five minutes is usually enough.

- **Broccoli:** Look for broccoli that's dark green or even purplish-green, but not yellow; yellowing means it's old. The florets should be compact and of even color. The leaves should not be wilted, and the stalks shouldn't be too fat and woody. Only buy broccoli that's kept cold; displayed at room temperature, broccoli loses taste and nutrients and becomes woody and fibrous. Store broccoli, unwashed, in a loosely closed plastic bag in the crisper drawer, and use within a few days. Wash broccoli carefully just before using. To help stems cook as quickly as florets, make one or two long cuts up through the stem just before steaming.

- **Cauliflower:** Choose any size head that is creamy white with compact florets. Brown patches and opened florets are signs of aging. Refrigerate cauliflower—unwashed, uncut, and loosely wrapped in plastic—in the crisper drawer; it'll keep two to five days. Keep the head upright to prevent moisture from collecting on the surface. To prepare cauliflower, remove the outer leaves, then break off the florets. Wash well under running water, and trim any brown spots.

Brussels Sprouts

- Fresh sprouts are available in fall and winter.
- Look for those with a pronounced green color and a tight, compact, firm head. The fewer yellowed, wilted, or loose leaves, the better. Smaller

heads will be more tender and flavorful. Try to pick ones of the same size so they'll cook evenly.

- Refrigerate sprouts in the cardboard container in which they're usually sold or in a loosely closed plastic bag; they should last a week or two.

- Just before cooking, dunk sprouts in ice water to debug them, then rinse under running water. Pull off any loose or wilted leaves. Trim the stem end just a little, then cut an "X" in the bottom of the stem, so it will cook as fast as the leaves.

- Steaming is the best way to cook sprouts: They will stay intact, their odor will be minimized, and their nutrients will be retained.

- Cook sprouts only until crisp-tender—when you can barely prick them with a fork—which usually takes 7 to 14 minutes depending on their size.

Cabbage

- Most cabbage is available year-round, but it's best in fall and winter.

- Choose a tight, compact head that feels heavy for its size. It should look crisp and fresh, with few loose leaves. The leafy varieties will not be as compact, of course, but be sure the leaves are green and stems are firm, not limp.

- Store cabbage, whole, in the crisper drawer of your refrigerator. Compact heads will keep uncut for a couple of weeks; leafy varieties should be used within a few days.

• To prepare cabbage, discard loose or limp outer leaves, then cut the head into quarters and wash.

• When cooking quarters, leave the core in, so the leaves will stay together.

• If shredding cabbage for coleslaw, core the cabbage just before using.

• For traditional beef and cabbage recipes, the long, slow cooking time is necessary only for the beef. The cabbage will taste best and retain the most nutrients if cooked until slightly tender but still crisp—about 10 to 12 minutes for wedges, 5 minutes for shredded. Red cabbage may require a few more minutes, and leafy varieties will probably need less time.

Putting Up a Stink

Cooking cruciferous vegetables, such as broccoli, cauliflower, brussels sprouts, and cabbage, can fill your home with a potent sulfur odor. But there are three steps you can take to help minimize or eliminate this side effect (assuming you find the aroma unpleasant). First, don't cook these vegetables in aluminum cookware; it will increase the odor. Second, soon after you start cooking, remove the top from the pot or pan for a minute or two, to help some of the smell dissipate. And finally, don't overcook these vegetables. Not only will it exacerbate their odor, it will make them mushy, pale, bland, and less nutritious.

Carrots

- Though sold year-round, carrots' true season is summer to fall.

- Look for firm, bright-orange carrots with smooth, root-free skin. Avoid limp carrots or those that are black near the top; they're not fresh.

> **The Key to Cooking Carrots**
>
> The nutrients in carrots are actually more usable by the body when the carrots are lightly cooked than when they are raw or overcooked. Cooking carrots only lightly is enough to break down their tough cell walls, but not enough to leach their nutrients, color, or flavor into the cooking water. Lightly cooked carrots are also sweeter than raw carrots.

- Choose medium-size carrots that taper at the ends; thicker carrots will taste tough. Early, or baby, carrots are more tender but less sweet than mature carrots.

- After purchase, clip off the greens so they won't suck moisture from the carrots; store both (if you plan to use the greens in soup stock) in perforated plastic bags in the crisper drawer. Carrots will keep for a few weeks, if cold enough, but the greens will be good only for a few days.

- Do not store carrots next to apples or pears, which produce ethylene gas that will rot the carrots.

- To prepare carrots, thoroughly scrub and rinse them to remove any soil or contaminants.

- As a root vegetable, the carrot tends to carry more pesticide residue than some other vegetables. To remove much of it, peel the carrot and cut off about a quarter-inch of the fat end.

Corn

- Available year-round, fresh corn is most abundant in summer.

- Look for fresh ears that have been kept in a cool place; warmth turns corn's natural sugar into starch, making it less sweet.

- Husks should be green, and visible kernels should be plump and tightly packed. The corn silk should be soft to the touch and gold in color.

- To test for freshness, pop a single kernel with your fingernail. The liquid that spurts out should be milky colored. If it's not, the corn could be either immature or overripe.

- Refrigerate corn as soon as you get it home; it quickly loses sweetness in warmer temperatures.

- When boiling fresh corn on the cob, don't add salt to the water, and don't overcook; both toughen the corn. Cook it for the shortest time possible—usually five to ten minutes.

Greens, Cooking

- Choose cooking greens with smooth, firm, green leaves. Small, young leaves are likely to be the least bitter and most tender. And be sure the seller kept them well chilled, or they'll be bitter. Avoid greens that are wilted, a sign of bitterness, or have brown-edged or slimy leaves.

- Unwashed greens store well for three to five days when wrapped in a damp paper towel and stored in an airtight plastic bag. The longer they are stored, however, the more bitter they become.

- Before cooking, wash greens well and remove tough stems; cook only the leaves.

- Cook greens with the lid off to prevent them from turning a drab olive color.

Greens, Salad

- Choose greens with firm, vividly colored leaves. Avoid wilted, brown-edged, or slimy leaves.

- Store salad greens in the refrigerator's crisper drawer, roots intact, in perforated plastic bags. Arugula and watercress will keep a day or two; endive will keep three to four days; radicchio will keep a week; and romaine, up to ten days.

- Before using, separate leaves and wash well. Swish small bunches in a bowl of water to clean.

Onions

- **Dry, or storage, onions** are common onions—
  yellow, white, or red—that do not require refrigeration. Choose firm bulbs with shiny, tissue-thin
  skins and dry, tight "necks." Avoid those that
  look dried out, are discolored, or have soft, wet
  spots. Dry onions will keep three to four weeks in
  a dry, dark, cool location; a hanging bag is ideal
  because it allows air to circulate. Light turns
  onions bitter, and dry onions will sprout and go
  bad if they get too warm, although
  refrigeration hastens deterioration,
  too. Once you cut an onion, wrap the
  rest in plastic, refrigerate, and use
  within a day or two.

- **Green onions** (also called spring onions) have
  small, white bulbs topped by long, thin, green
  stalks and are simply onions harvested at an
  immature stage. Although they are often sold as
  scallions, true scallions have no bulb, just long,
  slender, straight, green stalks. The terms green
  onions and scallions, however, are often used
  interchangeably. Look for green onions with
  bright-green tops that look crisp, not wilted. The
  bulbs should be well formed, with no soft spots.
  For more pungent aroma, choose those with fat-
  ter bulbs; for a sweeter taste, pick the smaller
  ones. Green onions must be refrigerated. They'll

keep best in a plastic bag in the crisper drawer. Use within two or three days. (Even after the tops have wilted and dried out, the bulb may be good for a few days more.)

> **Don't Cry**
> To keep your eyes dry when chopping onions, try slicing them under running water. If you are not so adept with your knife, try running cold water over your knife after every cut, or chill the onions for an hour before cutting them. To get the onion smell off your fingers, rub them with lemon juice or vinegar.

- Don't store onions next to potatoes, which give off a gas that causes onions to decay.

- To dice an onion easily: Peel it, then cut it in half (end to end) and trim the neck end, leaving the root end together. Place it flat-side down on a cutting board, and cut slices down to the root end without cutting through it. Then cut horizontally through the onion. Finally, cut the onion in slices parallel to the root end.

Peas, Green

- **Fresh green peas** are only available in April and May. Choose firm, bright-green pods that are plump but not large. Avoid yellow or blemished pods. A pound of pea pods yields about a cup of shelled peas. Wash green pea pods just before shelling and cooking. To shell, pinch off the ends, pull down the string on the inside, and pop out the peas.

- **Snow peas,** also called Chinese pea pods, are increasingly available fresh in supermarkets year-round. Look for shiny, flat pods. Pick the smallest ones for sweetness and tenderness. Avoid any cracked, overly large, limp, or dull pods. To prepare, just wash them and trim their ends.

- **Sugar snap peas,** available at farmer's markets in 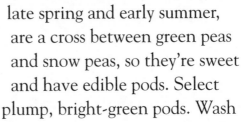 late spring and early summer, are a cross between green peas and snow peas, so they're sweet and have edible pods. Select plump, bright-green pods. Wash the pods, trim the ends, and remove the string from both sides of the pod.

- Fresh peas will keep for two or three days in the refrigerator, but the sooner you eat them the better they'll taste, because the sugar in them quickly turns to starch.

- Steam peas for a very short time—six to eight minutes, tops.

Peppers

- When choosing any type of pepper, look for a full shape with a glossy sheen. Avoid shriveled peppers or those with cracks or soft spots.

- **Sweet peppers** differ from hot peppers in that they lack capsaicin, the chemical responsible for the "fire" of hot peppers. Sweet peppers should feel heavy for their size, indicating fully developed, thick walls. Store them in the refrigerator crisper drawer in a plastic bag to hold in moisture. Green peppers can stay firm for a week, but the other colors will go soft after three or four days. Before using, thoroughly wash sweet peppers; use diluted, mild dish soap on supermarket peppers to help remove pesticides and wax. To core, cut into quarters, then trim away the stem and white membranes and wash away the seeds.

Colorful Peppers

You may be surprised to learn that a green bell pepper is simply a red, yellow, or purple pepper that isn't completely ripe. As it matures, it turns various shades of yellow-orange, until it is completely red (or purple). Because nongreen peppers are more ripe, they are more perishable and more difficult to keep fresh. Therefore, they carry a premium price. But many people favor their milder taste and vivid colors.

- **Hot peppers** come in over 200 varieties. Red ones, being more ripe, are usually hotter than green ones. Still, shape is a better indicator than color when trying to tell which peppers are hot and which are not. Rule of thumb: the smaller (or skinnier), the hotter. Hot

Warning!

When working with hot peppers, wear gloves and be sure to avoid touching your eyes. The peppers' oils are difficult to remove from the skin and will cause painful stinging and burning if they get in your eyes. Immediately after cutting hot peppers, wash all utensils and cutting boards—even the outer surfaces of the gloves, if they're not disposable—in hot, soapy water. And if you've eaten a hot pepper that's got more fire than you can handle, drink milk, which will help neutralize the burning, rather than water, which will only spread the fire throughout your mouth.

peppers keep best if refrigerated in a perforated paper bag. To dampen the fire of hot peppers, put on gloves and cut away the white membrane lining the inside, discarding the seeds as well, but be careful not to touch your eyes while working with hot peppers.

Potatoes

- Choose firm potatoes with no soft or dark spots. Skip green-tinged potatoes; they contain toxic alkaloids such as solanine. Also avoid any that are soft or sprouting; they're old.

- If you buy potatoes in a bag, open the bag right away and discard any rotting potatoes. A single bad potato can spoil a bagful.

- Store potatoes in a dark, dry, cool, ventilated location. Light causes production of solanine, and too

The Perfect Baked Spuds

To make dreamy baked potatoes, you have to use russet, sometimes called Idaho, potatoes—the large, long spuds with skin that's brown and dry. It's their lack of moisture, compared to other varieties, that makes them bake up fluffy. Prick the skin for an even fluffier potato. And if you're baking them in a conventional oven, don't wrap them in foil—unless you like mushy steamed potatoes.

much moisture causes rotting. But don't refrigerate potatoes, because their starch will convert to sugar, and don't store them with onions, because both will go bad more quickly. Mature potatoes keep for weeks; new potatoes only a week or so.

- Wash potatoes just before cooking. Scrub them well with a vegetable brush under running water. Cut out sprouts and bad spots.

Spinach

- Since curly- and smooth-leaved spinach taste the same, you can save time and effort by opting for the smooth variety, which is easier to clean.

- Choose spinach with dark-green, crisp leaves.

- Refrigerate spinach in a plastic bag; it should keep for three to four days.

- Wash spinach just prior to using. If you wash and then store it, the leaves will deteriorate rapidly.

- Wash all fresh spinach leaves carefully and thoroughly two or three times. Even the smallest speck of grit can ruin an otherwise perfect dish.

- Spinach should be simmered with very little water for only five to ten minutes.

Squash

- Both winter and summer squash are available all year, although winter squash is best from early fall to late winter.

- Look for smaller squash that are brightly colored and free of spots, bruises, and mold.

- The hard, protective skin of winter squash allows it to be stored longer than summer squash. It'll keep for a month or more in a dark, cool place. After you remove the seeds (peeling is optional), you can bake, steam, sauté, or simmer it.

Don't Eat the Great Pumpkin

Unless you plan to carve it into a jack-o'-lantern for Halloween, choose a small or medium-size pumpkin. Very large pumpkins tend to be tough and stringy. Also look for a pumpkin that is free of cracks or soft spots and has a deep-orange color. A whole pumpkin will keep well for up to a month if you store it in a cool, dry spot. If you cut it, wrap it and place it in the refrigerator; it should keep for about one week. To prepare a pumpkin for cooking, first wash any dirt from the surface. Cut away the skin; remove the seeds; then slice, dice, or cut the pulp into chunks.

- Summer squash will only keep for a few days in the crisper of the refrigerator.

Sweet Potatoes

- Though they are available year-round, peak season for freshly harvested sweet potatoes is mid-fall to late winter.

- The orange variety, with its thicker, darker skin and bright-orange flesh is much sweeter and moister than the yellow variety, which has thin, light-colored skin and pale yellow flesh that, when cooked, resembles a baking potato.

- Regardless of variety, look for potatoes that are small to medium in size with smooth, unbruised skin. Avoid those that have a white, stringy "beard" attached; it tells you the potato is over-mature and is probably tough and stringy.

- Though sweet potatoes look hardy, they actually are quite fragile and spoil easily. Any cut or bruise on the surface quickly spreads and ruins the whole potato. Do not refrigerate them; it speeds deterioration.

- For a change of pace, substitute the dry, yellow variety of sweet potato in just about any recipe that calls for white potatoes.

- Cook with the peel on to retain nutrients.

COOKING KNOW-HOW

In cooking, as in many other aspects of life, it's the little things that can truly make a difference. A decision as simple as when to add the cheese in a recipe can mean the difference between a sauce that's smooth and creamy and one that's stringy or rubbery. And the choice between cooking with or without a lid on the pot can dictate whether beans come out tender or tough. You won't necessarily find such cooking secrets on a recipe card or in a cookbook. But you will find them in this chapter—a collection of tricks of the trade that will have you frying, roasting, grilling, and even microwaving with greater skill and success.

Baking, Roasting & Braising

Casseroles

- For casseroles and acidic foods (such as those that contain tomatoes or citrus fruit or juice), glass and ceramic bakeware are good choices. They absorb heat more slowly and hold heat better than metal. Keep in mind, though, that when substituting glass bakeware in recipes that call for baking pans, you should reduce the oven temperature by 25°F.

Foiling Spills

If you want to use aluminum foil in the oven to catch spills, place it on the rack below the rack that's holding your food; don't line the rack that you're actually using (although you can spray the rack you're using with cooking spray to make spills easy to wipe off). Otherwise, you'll hinder the air circulation that's required to cook your food. For the same reason, use foil only on the part of the lower rack that is directly under the food; do not cover the entire rack.

Fish

- Fish won't stick to the pan during baking if you lay it on a bed of parsley, celery, and onions. This veggie bed also adds flavor.

Pizza

- For pizza with a crisper crust, choose a pan with a dark surface; for a softer crust, choose a shiny pan. Using a pizza pan with a bottom that's perforated with hundreds of small holes will also create a crisper and more evenly browned crust because the perforations allow moisture to escape.

Poultry

- It's best to baste a chicken only during the final 30 minutes of cooking. Sauce won't penetrate during the early cooking stages and may cause the chicken to brown too quickly.

- Some turkeys have pop-up timers that indicate doneness. However, they should not be considered a reliable indication of doneness. Use them only as a rough guide, and rely on a meat thermometer for an accurate indication of internal temperature (and thus doneness).

Roasts

- When roasting meat, minimize shrinkage by cooking it longer at a lower temperature. (Use with a meat thermometer to gauge doneness.)

- For cooking a roast, a shallow pan is best because it allows heat to circulate around the meat.

- Dropping a few tomatoes in the pan will help tenderize a pot roast. The acid helps break down the roast's stringy fibers.

- When carving roasts or other big pieces of meat, prevent stringiness and ensure tenderness by cutting across the

Let It Stand

Always let a roast stand at room temperature for 15 minutes after removing it from the oven. During this time, the temperature of the inside portion of the roast will increase by 5° to 10°F as heat is transferred from the hotter outside layers. The juices will "set" as the roast stands, resulting in less moisture loss when it is carved.

grain. Look for long, thin parallel fibers along the meat, and slice across them.

- The most efficient cookware for braising is a heavy pan that is not too much larger than the food being cooked.

Boiling, Simmering & Poaching

- Prevent messy boil-overs by inserting a toothpick horizontally between the pot and the lid so that steam can escape.

- If you're cooking rice and burn it slightly, you can remove the burned flavor by adding a heel from a loaf of fresh white bread and covering the pot for a few minutes.

- When cooking dried beans, don't allow the water to come to a boil; it will cause the beans to break apart and the skins to separate from the beans. Instead, maintain a gentle simmer.

- If you're cooking dried beans, and the recipe calls for salt or an acidic ingredient, such as tomatoes or wine, add these ingredients only during the last 30 minutes of

Don't Get Steamed

Here's a trick for preventing steam from scalding your wrists and hands when you drain boiling water from a pot: Turn on the cold-water tap before you begin pouring the hot water into the sink, and keep it on as you drain the pot.

cooking. Such ingredients tend to slow cooking and toughen dried beans.

- For a firmer texture when cooking dried beans, cook them uncovered. For a softer texture, cover the pot during cooking.

- When cooking lentils with an acidic ingredient, such as tomatoes or wine, you will need to increase the cooking time, possibly by as much as 10 or 15 minutes.

- When poaching eggs, add white vinegar to the poaching water (one tablespoon vinegar for every two cups water). This helps the egg whites to coagulate, resulting in a more compact shape.

- When adding parsnips to soups and stews, do so only during the last 10 to 15 minutes of cooking; otherwise, the parsnips will overcook and become mushy.

- If hot cooked pasta is not served immediately, it will become sticky. To separate it, just pour boiling water over the pasta.

Broiling

- If grease on your broiler catches fire, sprinkle salt or baking soda on the flames. Don't use flour as a fire extinguisher—it's explosive.

- When broiling uncoated chicken, you can keep it from drying out—and add a touch of flavor— by brushing it with lemon juice.

- Save time and effort when broiling sausages by putting the links on a skewer, so you can turn them all with one movement. They'll brown more evenly, too.

Frying

- To sauté food in butter, add the food just after the foam on the butter subsides.

- When sautéing boneless chicken breasts or other chicken pieces, use a shallow skillet if you want the chicken to come out crispy. A deep pan creates steam, causing a buildup of moisture and a loss of crispiness.

- If you chill chicken for an hour after flouring it for frying, the coating will adhere better.

- To get the odor out of a pan used for frying fish, sprinkle the pan with salt, pour hot water in it, let it stand for a while, and then wash as usual.

- Chicken livers won't splatter during frying if you perforate them with

Room to Fry
When frying meats, be careful not to overcrowd the pan. If there are too many pieces in the pan, the meat will actually steam rather than fry.

a fork beforehand. Puncture several holes in each.

- Clarified butter can be used to fry foods at a higher temperature than is possible when using regular butter, since it does not burn as easily. Clarifying is the process of slowly melting unsalted butter so that the water evaporates and the milk solids sink to the bottom. The clear liquid, or clarified butter, consisting of fat and flavor, is then carefully spooned or poured off.

- To add delicate flavor to an omelet, place a whole peeled garlic clove on the tines of the fork you use to beat the eggs.

- Overmixing pancake batter produces tough pancakes. Mix the batter only until the dry ingredients are moistened; the batter may still be lumpy.

- Resist the urge to press down on pancakes with a spatula during cooking. This will give the pancakes a dense and heavy texture.

Grilling

- To make turning food and cleaning your grill's grid easier, coat the clean grid with nonstick cooking spray prior to cooking. For best results (and professional-looking grill marks), oil the grid when it's hot—but don't do this while the grid is on the hot grill, because the oil droplets can easily catch fire. Instead, place the grid over the heat and allow it to get hot, then remove the grid from the grill wearing a heavy-duty grill glove and hold it a safe distance from the grill as you spray.

• When preparing your grill, create a coal-free area over which you can move food if flare-ups threaten to scorch it.

The Brick Trick

How do you get a split chicken or a butterflied game hen to cook evenly on the grill? Here's a quick and easy solution: Wrap a relatively clean brick in heavy-duty aluminum foil, and use it as a grilling weight. Placed on top of the poultry, the weight of the brick presses it down so the whole side is in contact with the grill. This trick also creates great grill marks!

• Leave the barbecue fork in the drawer and grab the long-handled tongs or spatula (or slip on a heavy-duty grill glove to use a short-handled version) to maneuver meat, fish, or poultry on the grill. Each time you turn or move the meat with a fork, you create more punctures that allow flavorful juices to escape during grilling.

• When you barbecue juicy meat, fat dripping on the hot coals can cause flames to flare up. Put out the flames by dropping lettuce leaves on the coals or by squirting water on the coals with a turkey baster or spray bottle.

- A handy way to hold shrimp and scallops on skewers while grilling is to use bacon strips. Thread one end of a raw bacon slice on the skewer, add a shrimp or scallop, bring the bacon through the skewer again, add another shrimp or scallop, and so on until you've loaded the skewer. As you grill the seafood on the skewer, the bacon will cook, too.

- Add zip to skewered vegetables by brushing them with Italian dressing instead of butter.

- If you plan to baste food during grilling using a sauce that contains sugar, honey, or tomato products, apply the sauce only during the last 15 to 30 minutes of grilling time; otherwise, the food will char. Basting sauces made from seasoned oils or butters may be brushed on throughout grilling.

- When preparing burgers for the grill, don't handle the meat too much. If you knead and squish the ground meat a lot, you compact it, and the patties won't be as juicy when they're cooked. Form the patties gently but firmly. Refrigerating them before grilling will help keep them firm.

- You've probably seen it done many times, but don't repeat this mistake: When you're cooking burgers on the grill, don't press on or flatten them with a spatula. This only squeezes out precious juices.

Beware Exploding Sausages!

If a sausage is heated too rapidly, steam can build up inside the casing. Steam will cause the casing to split or, worse, to explode like an over-inflated meat-filled balloon—not a pretty sight! The solution is to provide a few small release valves by pricking the sausage before cooking. But don't make the holes too big and don't make too many (don't keep piercing the sausage with a fork to turn it on the grill, for example), or too much juice will leak out and you'll end up with a dried-out sausage.

- How can you tell if the fish you're grilling is done? Peek. Use a knife and, at the thickest portion of the fish, gently part the flesh just enough to see inside. The flesh should be opaque all the way through. If you grill fish until it "flakes easily," you'll end up with dried-out fish that's difficult to remove from the grill in one piece. Overcooking is the worst thing you can do to fish.

Microwaving

- When cooking meats or vegetables in the microwave, cut them into uniform-size pieces to ensure even cooking.

- Remove large bones from meat before microwaving, because a dense bone may keep the area around it from cooking.

- Thick-skinned foods, such as potatoes, squash, and tomatoes, trap steam during microwave cooking, so pierce their skins before cooking to allow steam to escape.

- To make the chore of peeling foods like tomatoes, peaches, and apricots easier, microwave them on high power for 30 seconds, then allow them to stand for 2 minutes. Their peels will slip right off.

- Slicing an uncooked acorn or spaghetti squash can be a real challenge. Make it easier by softening the squash in the microwave first. Pierce the rind in a few places to allow steam to escape, then place the squash in the microwave and heat at high power for one to two minutes. Let it stand about three minutes, then slice.

- You can use your microwave to blanch almonds and remove their brown skins, which sometimes have a bitter taste. Place one cup water in a two-cup microwavable bowl; heat at high power two to two-and-a-half minutes until it comes to a boil. Add one cup of shelled whole almonds to the boiling water and heat on high power for one minute. Drain. When cool enough to handle, pinch the almonds at the wider end; they will pop right out of their skins.

• If you need to peel a large number of garlic cloves, here's a trick for loosening the papery skins: Place the whole head of garlic on a microwavable plate. Heat at high power for 20 to 30 seconds, turning the plate halfway through the heating time. Allow the garlic to stand for one minute, then peel.

• To get more juice from a lemon, lime, or other citrus fruit, pop it in the microwave on high power for 30 seconds.

• When heating a sandwich, roll, or other baked good in the microwave, wrap it in a paper towel. The towel will absorb moisture that would otherwise make the food soggy.

• There's no need to turn on your oven just to heat tortillas. They can be warmed and softened in the microwave instead. Just before using, stack the tortillas, wrap them in microwave-safe plastic wrap, and place them in the microwave. Heat them on high power for 30 to 60 seconds, turning them over and rotating them a quarter turn once during that time.

- Potato chips that have lost their crunch can be placed on paper towels in the microwave and heated briefly. The towels will restore the chips to crispness by absorbing the moisture that causes the stale texture.

- When reheating very dense food such as a bowl of mashed potatoes or a casserole, make a depression in the center to help it heat more evenly.

- Some foods cook better or heat more thoroughly when raised off the floor of the microwave. Elevating them allows the microwaves to reach the bottom center of the food. To elevate foods such as cakes, quiches, and meat loaves, place the food on an overturned microwavable bowl, plate, or ramekin. Elevating also helps when microwaving

It's All About Location

Frustrated by uneven heating of food in your microwave? Arranging the food more carefully can help. Remember: Food that is in the center of the dish or plate cooks more slowly than the food at the outer edge. So for more-even cooking or heating, place thicker, tougher food toward the outside of the dish and more delicate food toward the center. For example, when cooking broccoli or asparagus, place the stalks, which take longer to cook, toward the edge of the dish and the florets in the center. When reheating a plate of food, place thicker foods like meat or potatoes toward the outside of the plate. Place less dense, more delicate foods, such as fish, bread, or green beans, in the center.

small amounts of food, such as one or two table-spoons of butter. Raising the food places it closer to the center of the oven, where the microwaves are concentrated.

- When using the microwave to cook or reheat a dish that is to be topped with cheese, add the cheese to the dish only during the last few minutes of cooking time. This will help prevent overcooking, which causes cheese to become tough and rubbery.

Seasoning

- When doubling a recipe, do not automatically double the seasoning. It is better to use only 1½ times the original amount of seasoning and then taste the finished dish, making any necessary adjustments at that point.

- To cut basil leaves into thin strips, layer several leaves, with the largest leaves on the bottom. Roll up the leaves, starting at one side. Cut the roll crosswise into slices with a sharp knife. Separate slices into strips.

- To lengthen the storage time of fresh ginger, cover it with dry sherry in a small glass jar and store it in the refrigerator for as long as three months. Remove the ginger root from the sherry to use. It will have a slight sherry flavor. The ginger-flavored sherry may later be used for cooking, especially in stir-fried dishes.

- Do not store your herbs and spices above the range; it may seem like a convenient location, but the heat and moisture will cause their flavors to deteriorate more quickly. Store dried herbs and spices in a cool, dry place in tightly covered, lightproof containers.

- When herbs are dried, their oils become more pungent. Therefore, as a general rule of thumb when substituting dried herbs for fresh, use one teaspoon dried herbs in place of one tablespoon chopped fresh herbs.

- Papaya seeds can be dried, ground, and used as a spice or as a meat tenderizer. The flesh of the papaya also has a natural tenderizing effect, so it can be pureed and used to marinate meats.

Heavy-Metal How-To

If a recipe suggests a heavy saucepan and you don't have one, place a lightweight saucepan in a skillet. The extra layer of metal will provide just the right amount of insulation.

- To preserve its quality, vinegar should be stored in a cool, dark place. An opened bottle of commercially produced vinegar will keep for six months; unopened vinegar will keep indefinitely.

BAKING WISDOM

Baking can be pure pleasure, especially when the recipe turns out just right. But like any other human endeavor, little things can and do go wrong along the way, and the best-laid plans can collapse like a soufflé after the oven door's been slammed. Experienced bakers have been there before, and they've discovered secrets and devised strategies to prevent or fix lots of the little problems that can spoil both the baked goods and the baking experience. You'll find some of that know-how collected here. And whether you're a budding baker or you've been whipping up cakes and pies for years, you're sure to find some new tricks that can enhance your baking prowess and pleasure.

Bakeware

- When choosing metal bakeware, buy pans of the heaviest weight and best quality you can afford—they will produce better results and last longer.

- Aluminum pans are excellent conductors of heat, producing uniform baking and browning. However, aluminum can react with acids in food, affecting the flavor and color of the food and damaging the pan. While this is not generally a

 problem with baked goods, aluminum bakeware should not be used for marinating or for baking dishes that contain citrus fruit or juice.

- For acidic foods (such as those that contain citrus fruit or juice), glass and ceramic bakeware are good choices. They also absorb heat more slowly and hold heat better than metal.

- When substituting glass bakeware in recipes that call for using (metal) baking pans, reduce the oven temperature by 25°F.

- Stainless steel is nonreactive and easy to clean, but it is a poor conductor of heat.

- Metal pans with shiny exteriors are best for cakes, because they produce tender, lightly browned, delicate cake crusts.

- Dull or dark-surfaced metal pans absorb heat more quickly than shiny pans, shorten baking time, and produce crisp, brown crusts that are desirable for breads (except for quick breads, which do better in shiny metal pans) and pies. Reduce the oven temperature by 25°F when using pans with dull or dark finishes to prevent overbrowning and crisp crusts.

- When buying a baking sheet (also called a cookie sheet), be sure to know the dimensions of your

Gelatin with a Kick

For an interesting, adult twist on a basic gelatin dessert, mix the gelatin with one cup boiling water, then add one cup red wine. Refrigerate at least four hours before serving.

oven. A baking sheet should fit on an oven rack with at least one inch between the sheet and the oven wall on all sides; otherwise, heat circulation will be hampered.

- Choose cookie sheets made of heavy-gauge, *shiny* aluminum; they are best for producing evenly baked and browned cookies. Darker cookie sheets absorb more heat and can cause overbrowning or burning.

- Using insulated baking sheets—the ones with an air pocket between their layers—to bake cookies will slightly lengthen the baking time needed and will result in cookies that are not quite as crisp as those made on regular baking sheets.

- When choosing a pie pan or pie plate, keep in mind that glass or dark-metal pie pans produce a crisp, golden crust, while shiny-aluminum pans produce a paler crust.

Breads, Muffins & Biscuits

- Yeast dough should rise only until it is doubled in size. Allowing it to rise beyond that point will result in inferior texture. Begin checking yeast dough 10 to 15 minutes early for signs of sufficient rising. Always preheat the oven before rising is completed.

- To test if yeast dough has risen properly, lightly press two fingertips about half an inch into the dough. The dough is ready if an indentation remains when you pull your fingers away.

- Mix muffins just until the dry ingredients are moistened; some lumps may remain, and that's perfectly okay. Overmixing will give your muffins a tough texture.

- Knead biscuit dough lightly (10 to 12 times) to bring it together for shaping. Too much kneading will make biscuits mealy and tough.

- When you begin a dough-kneading project or some other messy, hands-on task in the kitchen, keep a gallon-size plastic bag propped open near your telephone. That way, if you get a call during the task, you can simply slide your messy or sticky hand into the bag and answer the call without getting the receiver all gooey. (This is a "handy" trick to know when you're gardening or transplanting houseplants, painting around the house, or doing other messy DIY projects.)

Cakes

- If you're having difficulty removing cake layers from baking pans—which can happen if you

Dropping Like *Raisins?*

To prevent raisins from sinking to the bottom of a cake or muffin batter, toss them with a little of the flour used in the recipe. If the raisins are clumped together, separate them with your fingers first, so all the raisins get thoroughly coated with flour.

allow the layers to cool too long in their pans—simply place the pans in a preheated 350°F oven for three to five minutes, then turn the layers out onto wire racks.

- Cutting one layer of a layer cake into two thinner layers can be tricky, but you can do it with unflavored dental floss. First, insert toothpicks horizontally into the cake at the cutting line. Then, holding a long length of dental floss tightly between your hands, start at the far side and pull the floss toward you, using the toothpicks as a guide.

- For easier frosting and decorating, place cooled cake layers in the freezer for 30 to 45 minutes before frosting.

- To make an easy and inexpensive cake-icing tool, put the icing in a quart-size plastic bag (but don't fill the bag more than about halfway). Force the icing into one corner of the bag by carefully

Be Quick About It

Once you fill a baking pan with cake batter, immediately place it in a preheated oven. Cake batter should not sit out before baking, because chemical leaveners begin working as soon as they are mixed with liquids, and the air in foam batters will begin to dissipate. In addition, once you put the pan of cake batter into the oven, do not open the oven again during the first half of the baking time. Cold air will interfere with the rising of the cake.

squeezing the bag and pushing the icing down toward the corner. With one hand, carefully twist the top of the bag once or twice, just above the level of the icing, to keep the icing from shooting out the top. Then snip off a small piece of the corner. Guide this "tip" with one hand as you use your other hand to continue twisting and gently squeezing the bag from the top down. With practice, you'll be able to make designs and even write names. (This trick works for whipped cream, too.)

- To keep an eight-inch round cake from sticking to the pan, line the pan with a flattened, paper coffee filter before pouring in the batter. The filter works just like paper cupcake cups.

- When making a chocolate cake from a box, try adding a teaspoon of instant coffee to the water that's called for. You'll create an elegant-tasting mocha cake!

- Use a paper coffer filter to make a "fancy" stencil for powdering the tops of cakes and pastries. Fold the filter in half, then in half again, and snip a design into it—much like you would to make paper snowflakes. Unfold the filter, apply a light coat of cooking spray to one side, set the filter sprayed-side down on top of the cake, and sprinkle powdered sugar over it. Then gently lift off the filter, and voilà!

- When you need to cover an iced cake or iced cupcakes, first spray one side of the plastic wrap with cooking spray; that way, the icing won't stick to the wrap and ruin the decoration.

- Marshmallows make excellent quick frosting for cupcakes. When baking cupcakes, add a marshmallow to the top of each one about one minute before they're done baking. The marshmallows will melt into instant frosting!

- To prevent your homemade cheesecake from cracking, do not overmix the batter; beat just until the mixture is blended.

Cookies & Brownies

- When making cookies, be sure to preheat the oven for 10 to 15 minutes; otherwise, your cookies won't bake properly.

- When you're making shaped, or molded, cookies, such as spritz cookies or madeleines, do not substitute margarine for butter. Margarine produces a softer dough, so your cookie dough may not hold its shape.

- To make it easier to handle cookie dough that you will be rolling out and dividing with cookie cutters, chill the dough in the refrigerator for about an hour before you plan to use it. Then remove only enough dough from the refrigerator to work with at one time.

- To minimize sticking of dough when using cookie cutters, spray the cutters with cooking spray or dip them in flour.

- To keep a log of cookie dough round during slicing, roll it a quarter turn every four or five slices.

- For easy removal of brownies and bar cookies (and no cleanup!), line the baking pan with foil,

When the Cookies Crumble

Does your recipe call for graham-cracker or cookie crumbs? Save yourself plenty of mess by slipping the crackers or cookies into a quart- or gallon-size plastic bag (if you use the resealable kind, do not seal the bag all the way across, because you'll want air to be able to escape easily) and rolling your rolling pin over the bag. Even your rolling pin will stay clean. Plus, if you don't use all of the crumbs right away, you can just seal the bag and store the crumbs for the next recipe that calls for them.

leaving at least three inches hanging over on each end. Once the goodies are done cooking and have cooled, lift them—foil and all—off the pan and place them on a cutting board. Remove the foil and cut the treats into pieces.

- If you forgot to line your cookie sheet with foil, and your cookies are now stuck to it, grab a length of unflavored dental floss. Hold the floss taut with both hands, and slide it under the cookies to dislodge them without breaking them apart or scratching your cookie sheet.

- Cookies that are uniform in shape and size will finish baking at the same time. To make drop cookies that are uniformly shaped, scoop the dough using a small ice-cream scoop—the kind with a release bar is best. The handiest sizes are 40, 50, and 80 (the size is usually stamped on the release bar).

- If you need to reuse cookie sheets when you're baking several batches of cookies at a time, be sure to let the sheets cool completely before placing another round of dough on them. Otherwise, the dough will soften and begin to spread before you put it in the oven, which will affect the texture and shape of the finished cookies.

- For easy cleanup when rolling out cookie dough, put the dough on a sheet of waxed paper that has been placed directly on the countertop or table-top. Lightly spray or sprinkle water on the countertop first to keep the waxed paper from sliding.

- Need an easy glaze for bar cookies? Sprinkle them with chocolate chips immediately after baking, then cover with foil. You can use toothpicks to keep the foil from sticking to the chocolate. After three or four minutes, remove the foil and spread the melted chips over the bars.

- To give your cookies color and sparkle, add a little food coloring to plain gelatin powder and sprinkle the powder on your fresh-baked cookies.

- Be sure cookies have cooled completely before you store them. If cookies are put away warm, the steam they produce will cause all the cookies in the container to become soggy and soft.

- Never store different kinds of cookies in the same container; their flavors and textures can change.

- To keep moist cookies soft, store them with two or three thick apple slices in a tightly covered container for a day or two, then remove the apple. Apple slices may also be added to a storage container to soften stale or overbaked cookies.

- Don't assemble sandwich cookies more than two days before you need them, or they'll get soggy. It's best to fill them the day they'll be eaten.

Ingredients

- Toasting nuts enhances their flavor. Simply spread nuts in a single layer on a jelly-roll pan and bake in a preheated 325°F oven for eight to ten minutes or until lightly toasted, stirring several times. Allow the nuts to cool before using them.

- For fruit desserts with the best flavor, always use fully ripened fruit.

- To measure flour accurately, spoon it into a measuring cup until the cup is overflowing. Then sweep across the top of the cup with a straight-edged metal spatula. Do not directly scoop the flour with the measuring cup or tap the cup on the counter, because this will compact the flour and result in an inaccurate measure.

- When it's time to restock your supply of flour, use up all of the flour remaining in the container first, and clean the container thoroughly, before you add any of the new flour. Be sure the container is airtight, too. And store it in a cool, dry place at room temperature (do not refrigerate flour).

Tackling a Brown-Sugar Boulder

It's happened to all of us at some point: You reach into the box to scoop out some brown sugar, and you hit something that feels like concrete. Instead of trying to chip away at the brown-sugar boulder, try one of these tips:

- Place a cut piece of apple in the bag or container and close it tightly for one or two days, then remove the apple, and the sugar should be easier to work with.
- A quicker option is to place a piece of dampened paper towel in the box of brown sugar, close the box tightly, and heat the whole thing in a microwave set on high for 20 or 30 seconds.

- Store baking powder and baking soda in a cool, dry place. Replace them after six months to ensure that your baked goods rise properly.

- Before dusting a cake or other baked good with powdered sugar, be sure the baked good has cooled completely first. Otherwise, the sugar will dissolve and disappear.

- If a recipe calls for molasses but does not specify a type, dark or light may be used. Dark has a more robust, slightly less sweet flavor than light. Don't use blackstrap molasses; it's a little bitter.

- Before measuring molasses or other sticky liquids, lightly coat the measuring cup with nonstick cooking spray so the molasses will slide out easily.

- For an easy way to drizzle chocolate, melt it in a resealable plastic bag in the microwave. Then cut a small corner off the bottom of the bag and gently squeeze it to drizzle the chocolate over food.

• In recipes, cocoa powder may be used in place of unsweetened chocolate. For every ounce of unsweetened chocolate needed, substitute three tablespoons unsweetened cocoa powder plus one tablespoon butter, margarine, or shortening.

When Chocolate Goes Gray

When chocolate is stored at too high a temperature, white or gray streaks or mottling—called "bloom"—may appear on the surface. This indicates that the cocoa butter has separated, come to the surface, and crystallized. It does not, however, mean the chocolate is spoiled. The cocoa butter will recombine when the chocolate is melted.

• To minimize lumps when using cocoa powder to make beverages or syrups, combine it with the sugar in the recipe before adding the liquid.

• If your cream is buttery from overbeating, carefully whisk in more whipping cream, one tablespoon at a time, until the yellow curds disappear.

• The flavor of extracts (such as vanilla and almond) fades quickly when cooked, so let foods cool slightly before adding extracts.

• Because of their high oil content, poppy seeds tend to become rancid if stored at room temperature. Refrigerated, they'll keep up to six months.

Pies & Pastry

- Rolling out a pastry crust is a breeze if you use a canvas pastry cloth. Just dust the cloth generously with flour and roll out the dough to the approximate size that you need. Always wash the cloth after use.

- To decrease mess when you're making a pie, try kneading and rolling out the dough inside a gallon-size plastic bag.

- When making pastry, spray all of the spatulas, spoons, and mixing bowls with cooking spray first to keep the process moving smoothly and to make cleanup easier.

- Are you tired of trying to remove baked-on messes from the inside of your oven or racing to silence the smoke alarm when yesterday's spillover begins to burn on your oven rack today? Spread a sheet of aluminum foil—cut so it's just a bit larger than the footprint of the baking pan—on the oven rack below the rack holding your baking pan. Do not, however, spread foil on the bottom of the oven.

- To add a shiny, golden glaze to the top crust of a fruit pie, brush with milk or an egg wash of one beaten egg and one tablespoon water just before baking. For a darker, glossier color, substitute cream for the milk or an egg yolk for the whole egg. Delay brushing the decorative edge of the pie until the last 15 to 20 minutes of baking to avoid overbrowning.

- If a piecrust is browning too quickly, cover the edges with strips of foil or cut the bottom out of a foil pie pan and invert it over the pie.

- Need to prebake a pie or tart crust before filling it but don't have any metal or ceramic pie weights? No problem. Rice or dried beans from your pantry will do. First, prick the shell all over with a fork, then line it with foil or parchment and fill it with dried beans or rice. Bake the shell as directed, removing the liner and beans or rice during the last few minutes of baking to allow the crust to brown. The beans or rice can be cooled, stored in an airtight container, and reused in the same way, but they should not be cooked and eaten.

- To thicken fruit-pie fillings, replace the flour called for with an equal amount of quick-cooking tapioca.

- The two secrets to flaky, tender pastry? Minimize your handling of the dough, and be sure to distribute the fat evenly throughout the dough.